# Your Faith
# ISLAM

*By Harriet Brundle*

*You can find the **bold** words in this book in the Glossary on page 24.*

# PHOTO CREDITS

# CONTENTS

Page 4-5    *What is Religion?*

Page 6-7    *What is Islam?*

Page 8-9    *Allah and Muhammad*

Page 10-11  *The Qur'an*

Page 12-13  *Places of Worship*

Page 14-15  *Prayer in a Mosque*

Page 16-17  *Mecca*

Page 18-19  *The Hajj*

Page 20-21  *Ramadan and Eid*

Page 22-23  *Facts about Islam*

Page 24     *Glossary and Index*

©2016
Book Life
King's Lynn
Norfolk PE30 4LS

Written by:
Harriet Brundle

Designed by:
Drue Rintoul

ISBN: 978-1-910512-93-7

A catalogue record for this book
is available from the British Library.

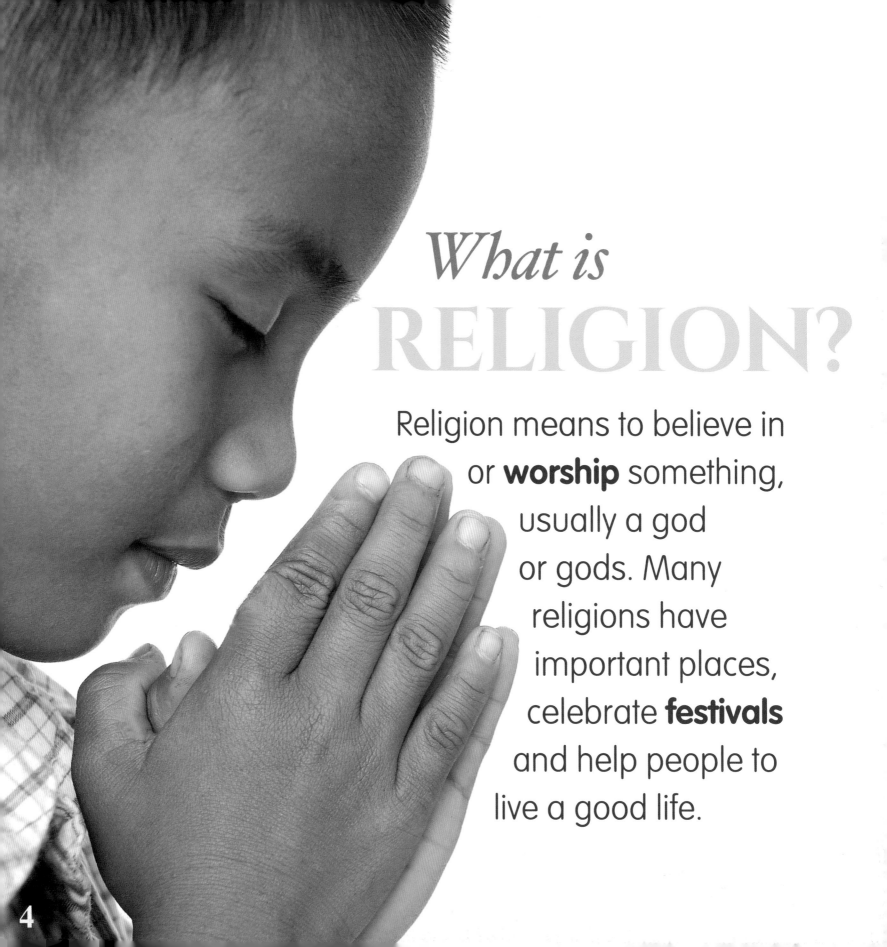

# What is RELIGION?

Religion means to believe in or **worship** something, usually a god or gods. Many religions have important places, celebrate **festivals** and help people to live a good life.

4

There are lots of different religions. Some of the religions with the largest amount of followers are Christianity, Islam, Hinduism and Sikhism.

CHRISTIANITY

ISLAM

HINDUISM

SIKHISM

# *What is* ISLAM?

Islam is a religion that began over one thousand years ago. It is the second largest religion in the world.

People who follow Islam are called Muslims and they believe in one God, called Allah. It is very important to Muslim people to follow Allah's word.

# Allah and MUHAMMAD

Muslims believe that a man called Muhammad was chosen to hear Allah's words. Allah spoke to Muhammad and told him how to practise his **faith**.

Muhammad spread these words to many other people. They were written down in a book called the Qur'an so that all Muslims could read them.

# The QUR'AN

The Qur'an is a special book for Muslims and it is written in a language called Arabic. Muslims believe they are the words of Allah.

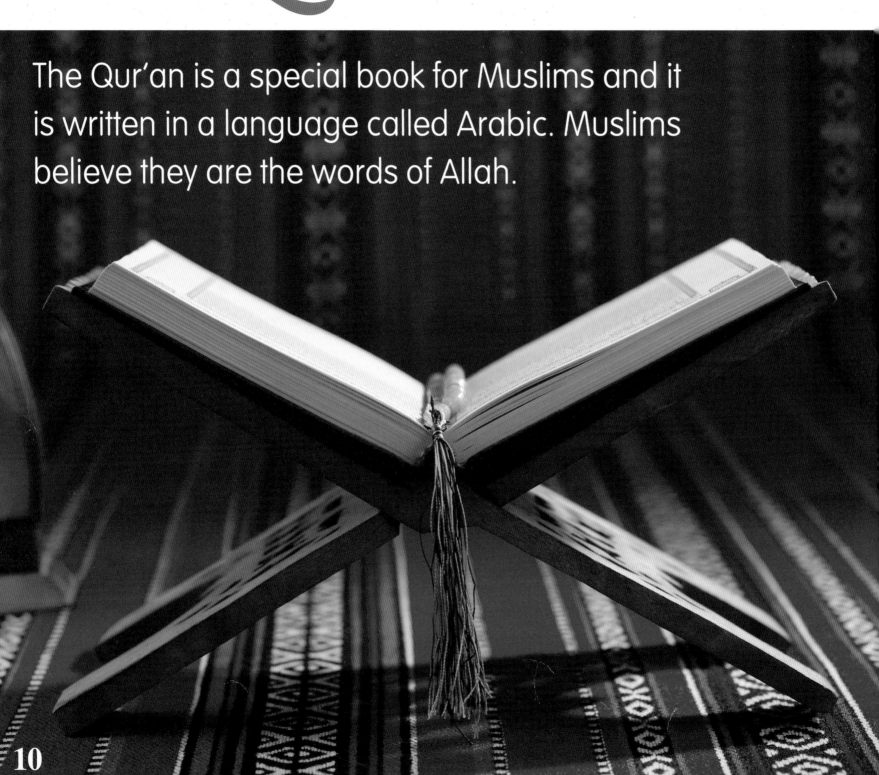

The Qur'an is an important part of life for Muslim people. Parts of the Qur'an are read out loud when Muslims pray.

*A person who has **memorised** the whole Qur'an is called a hafiz.*

# Places of WORSHIP

Muslim people can worship Allah in a mosque. A mosque usually has tall towers, called minarets, which can be seen from far away.

It is important for Muslims to pray five times every day because this is one of the **Five Pillars of Islam**.

*There are no seats inside a mosque because everybody kneels on the floor to pray.*

13

# Prayer in
# A MOSQUE

Muslims believe that when they pray they should be clean, so they wash their face, neck, arms, hands and feet.

Before going into a mosque, everyone must take off their shoes. This shows **respect** for Allah.

# MECCA

The city of Mecca is found in the country of Saudi Arabia. It is one of the most important places for Muslims.

*Muslim people believe that Muhammad was born in Mecca.*

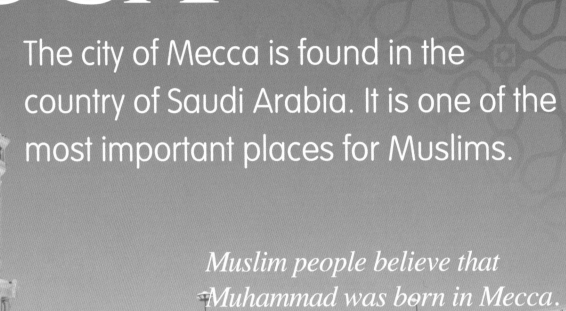

Inside every mosque there is a special place which shows the **direction** of Mecca. When Muslims pray, they must always face Mecca.

# The HAJJ

Muslim people must make the journey to Mecca once in their lifetime, as long as they have enough money to and are well. This trip is called the Hajj.

*The Hajj is one of the Five Pillars of Islam.*

There is a large building in the middle of Mecca that Muslim people must walk around seven times.

*This building is called the Kaaba.*

# Ramadan and EID UL-FITR

Muslims believe that it was in the Islamic month of Ramadan that Allah first spoke to Muhammad. To show their faith, Muslim people **fast** for the whole month.

Eid ul-Fitr is a festival that marks the end of Ramadan.
Eid ul-Fitr means that people no longer need to fast.

*Muslims eat together and share gifts.*

# Facts about ISLAM

**1** To become a Muslim, a person must say the Shahada: "There is no god but Allah; Muhammad is the messenger of God". Saying the Shahada is one of the Five Pillars of Islam.

**2** Muslim people must give money to the poor and needy. This is one of the Five Pillars of Islam.

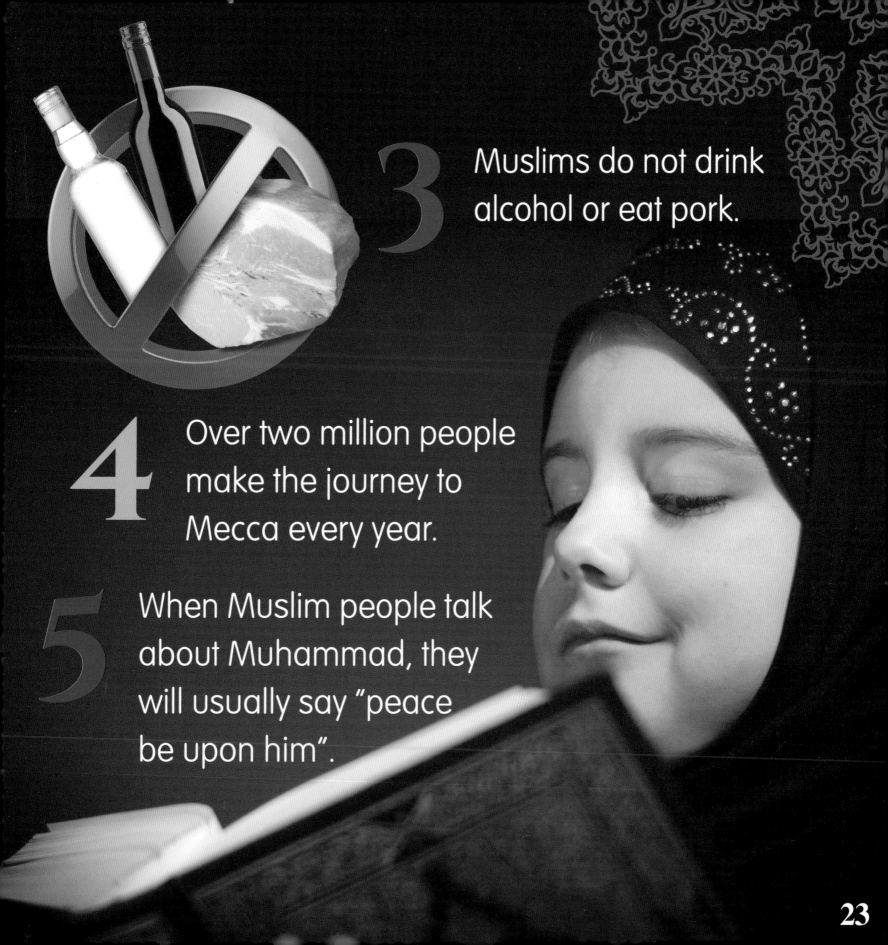

**3** Muslims do not drink alcohol or eat pork.

**4** Over two million people make the journey to Mecca every year.

**5** When Muslim people talk about Muhammad, they will usually say "peace be upon him".

# GLOSSARY

*Direction* the position that someone or something faces

*Faith* trust or confidence in someone or something

*Fast* not eating or drinking between sunrise and sunset

*Festivals* when people come together to celebrate special events or times of the year

*Five Pillars of Islam* five acts that Muslim people must do

*Memorised* to have learnt something by heart

*Respect* to show care

*Worship* to show a feeling of respect

# INDEX

Allah 7, 8, 10, 12, 15, 20, 22

Five Pillars of Islam 13, 18, 22

Mosque 12, 13, 14, 15, 17

Pray 11, 13, 14, 17

Qur'an 9, 10, 11

Religion 4, 5, 6

Worship 4, 12